IT'S THE SUGAR, SUGAR

By the same author

Acting Like a Girl (2019)
The Orlando Files (2018)
Who Sleeps at Night (2017)
One Last Border: Poetry for refugees with Hazel Hall and Moya Pacey (2015)
Projected on the Wall (2015)

IT'S THE SUGAR, SUGAR

SANDRA RENEW

RECENT
WORK
PRESS

It's the Sugar, Sugar
Recent Work Press
Canberra, Australia

Copyright © Sandra Renew, 2021

ISBN: 9780648936770 (paperback)

 A catalogue record for this
book is available from the
National Library of Australia

Cover image: © Julie Watkins, photo 3043873 Dreamstime.com
Cover design: Recent Work Press
Set by Recent Work Press

recentworkpress.com

SS

To Tikka

Contents

there's a love story here

North of Proserpine, in FNQ, boiling in the sugar towns,
love comes as regular as the arrowing of sugarcane flowers

glorious then, when the girls are out on tractors,
grimed and brown in their navvy singlets, old felt hats

cane fields burned and ploughed back in—
it's the sugar sweet, cloying, promising wonders

in the end destroyed in a blaze seen by ships passing at sea,
smoke-drift warning, vision-clouding haze

and the brief hit, slept off in the sweat-tangled sheets
hemmed in by wall mould, and bug-eyed gecko voyeurs

sticky

December 11th heats us up, drools darkness ...
most popular day of the year for a break-up

spread sugar and beer on a tree trunk at night
to catch the moths circling, frantic in the lamplight

we watch each other eat mangoes, yellow then gold
over-the-top umber sticky liquid sugar

keeping us together

Legs

She spent too much time that morning, inside the cicadas' roar, cutting the legs off the bed. The cutting wasn't the problem once she'd found a curved, rough-toothed hand-saw in the shed out the back. But then she went round and round trying to get the legs the same length. The bed got lower and lower and still wobbled sharply when she sat on it.

The floor was untrustworthy, so she micro-moved the bed until a position was found that suited all legs, uneven floorboards and her stab at sophistication in having a bedframe low to the floor.

Her girlfriend's dog had been out and come back. Had rolled in the rotting bagasse pile left over from our own efforts at crushing some sugar out of a stand of cane. Had tested the bed, standing four-square when the bed proved unstable, then tracked off to a more reliable spot on the verandah.

Under the mango tree, outside her window, the cane cutters smoked, held their beer bottles with elbows stiff against any inadvertent intimacy, legs braced in boots anchored wider than their shoulders, one pinching a rollie, one with his thumb hitched in the belt of his shorts. "You can put bigger wheels on it. It'll bloody rock it, mate, then it'll have legs", and that was about a ute or a truck or a bloke-associated accessory.

The cane that year was six feet tall, planted so close to the house she could lean out, wrest a stalk from the stand and warn off any bat or spider or rodent that lusted after a comfy corner in the hot, airless house.

the thing

The smoke and sugar affected everything, provided a cosy, embracing ambience, totally unrequired in the tropical heat, for a short, off-season ... what to call it?
Not a *romance* with love and longing and hope, and yearning and inappropriate happiness ...
Not a *lust fest* of expedient proximity ...
Not an *affair*, or a *liaison*, with implications of middle-class gentility ...
More than a careless long weekend ...
It was a short, off-season *thing* that she remembered from time to time through the next harvest, and twenty years on ...

retro-chic chick

the currency of cost is not lost on me, but paid in salt—
debited in sweat, lost in tears, credited in blood no longer needed

salt is leached from me with every thirst and water overdose in tropical
humidity, taking with it, in drops of sweat oozing from skin, eye watering sting,
all that is vital.

an original cross-dresser, sodium chloride goes anywhere and everywhere, with
every dishing up, dishing-it-out, temperature-raising, adrenalin provocation.

salt in translation is still salt
in the mouth, chemical
under the microscope, crystalline

she feeds her body sugar

she feeds her body sugar
craves sweetness hit and mood lift
when Mars Bar and soft drink seduce her
she feeds her body sugar
patisserie and ice-cream array ensnare, her
bloodstream screams in sugar crash, glucose shift
she feeds her body sugar
craves sweetness hit and mood lift

Cane train blues

silent mill and siding, cane trains hibernating
tropics suffocating, tracks closed due to missing bridge
narrow gauge sleepers for white ants off-season tasting
silent mill and siding, cane trains hibernating
no quiet traffic, bicycles or walkers stopped at level crossings, waiting
cicadas reach crescendo unconcerned for new season haulage
silent mill and siding, cane trains hibernating
tropics suffocating, tracks closed due to missing bridge

Burdekin snow

red-eyed cutters grimed in sugar smoke
flush snakes, spiders, possums, mice and rats
that run from flame and blade. Sweat slicks the bodies of the blokes,
red-eyed cutters grimed in sugar smoke,
indentured workers, from island homes, spirits not quite broke.
Flames and soot and molten heat, an acrid tableau that's
red-eyed cutters grimed in sugar smoke
flushing snakes and spiders, possums, mice and rats.

It's the sugar, Sugar

When she's high she calls me 'Sugar',
it's the glucose talking, not the dope.
She's gorgeous, wild, a real looker,
when she's high she calls me 'Sugar',
not sweet, no-one will mess with her ...
life with her, you're on a tightrope.
When she's high she calls me 'Sugar',
it's the glucose talking, not the dope

smartarses

when the rain turns into sugar
they think they'll live forever
still be laughing, high, too clever
when the rain turns into sugar
drunk on each other, wherever
they find tomorrow's lover
when the rain turns into sugar
they think they'll live forever

Bobby Dazzler and the
tractor pulling contest

they came by ute to woo her
Sugar Princess of the Festival
seductress of the Sugar Country Motor Inn

dazzled by her beauty, centrefold or pin-up
check her out, you bloody beauty
bloody oath and bloody ripper, she's a bottler

I didn't warm to our Sugar Princess
until I saw her tractor, a Massey Ferguson
modified from vintage true. They left by ute, deflated,

when they saw her high on mishaps, fails,
fires, wild rides and the carnage of the
utes and tractors, everyone was high on pulling-fuel

good onya mate, a toughened Princess
goddess, fair dinkum Venus for our modern day
hot as   a true-blue bobby dazzler

Sixteen lovers and the moon

Fair enough, the sun keeps coming up, and moon remains the great complicator.

The politics of the moon, ebb and flow, wax and wane. It's all myth, like a magneto providing current for ignition, when wheels only turn by themselves on a down slope, dominos only fall after you flick the line with your thumb, waves only roll because the moon disturbs them.

We go on as if we had not happened, never cooking a Sunday dinner, grilling something from frozen. Sangers if there's bread enough, fresh enough. Pie and chips from the takeaway (on the TV, Nigella winces). Something about chicken wings, instant noodles, smoky haze from a failed kitchen, cooking lessons for instant coffee and cinnamon toast.

Well you might wonder, how, now, is my state of mind, sixteen lovers later? And, of concern in the equation, what is the modus operandi of the sixteen lovers, possessive determiners, same side always presented to the Earth? Flow is not water, think dominos falling, the *effect* of falling moves from one to the other. Taking the moon as the standard, I measure relationships in months, more than a long weekend.

Timescape outing

What was it like? you ask, your coming out?
Mate I say mate
it was both the first time and the last time
two girlfriends, best friends, and lovers time
a latest move from limbo—

it takes a lifetime, a daily jive to keep ahead
of social protocol, to place you
as a dyke, a straight chick, or a weirdo

but mate, there was this one time,
a small-town carnival, a rodeo
the timescape of an outing
in a landscape of abrasion.
I remember old growth spinifex,
like all the bridges I had known,
was burning—
anonymity had forever
been my one safe haven from predation, a habitat protection
from intense boom events, drama queen spiking
after rain inundation—
from bad news, not up to long-held anticipation
no queues of girls, no welcome arms
no two of us 4eva, no graffiti proclamations
and, of course, I ran the gauntlet, of assault, abuse
and dickhead complication!

but mate, she was there, mate, the girl,
in bright blue shirt, Akubra, riding boots, roping gloves,
her fancy belt with trophy buckle, pocketknife,
sitting easy on her dancing muscled Waler
a wink is flashed, she tips her brim,
a see-you-later-in-the-pub grin ...

it was spinifex meets desert pea
it was the best time, the only time, a can't ever be undone line,
shining up my desert boots (nah they're suede, mate)
all tooled up for showing off,

and there we were, together in the public bar
with a rum and beer chasers, hands entwined
while the punters I was afraid of ignored us both completely
and we sat together, under radar, in the shouting and the roar

so, mate, I say mate, it was the best time and the only time
that coming out together time!

Truck

Birdsville to Bedourie is a short stretch of bitumen when you measure it against the total kilometres of highway available for coming out in this empty country, but it's long enough.

Thanks for stopping, Driver—What's your name, anyway? Aaah, Felicity—you're known as Feral? That's good, that's interesting ...

So, Feral, I saw you earlier, back at the truck-stop, you know, we both tried for water from the taps in the Ladies (it has a picture of a woman in a ball gown so I'm pretty sure you knew it was 'our' room). Yes, I know it could have been much improved with a bit of a clean, but who is left to do it? I quit the café job last Monday, on the off-chance. Can I ask you something Feral? In a monster truck like this, where do you sleep? Oh, you don't?

My tattoo is just wishful thinking at the moment, Feral, but I love what you've done with the ink—on-coming headlights making movies of your arms ... so cool!

Those multi-coloured wings, do they go right over your shoulders and arms? The double women's sign on the back of your neck, I get it, the personal is political! And those rainbow stars are just floating up your neck into your hairline, wow ...

OK, of course I can do a smokable rollie—where's the Drum and papers? No, I'm not a smoker myself, but it's not a deal-breaker when you get down to it. Is it lonely here on the road, Feral? Is someone waiting for you in the Isa? Yes, I do talk a lot when I'm not sure what the hell I'm doing. Yes, I will shut up now.

You've done something with your hair since you were through here on Monday, number 4 clippers, I guess, really makes a statement. What, stalking you? No, that's a big word!

Feral, what's the nightlife like for a girl in the Isa? ...
Of course, I'm up for it. I'm out here, aren't I ... ?

Jeep

You can drive it up a wall says the salesman at Dominion Motors in Brisbane, breathless with adrenalin and testosterone. *You can drive it under water.*

In 1976 we had one of those Willys MBs, dirty green with white military numbers painted on the bonnet, Hurricane F-head, four-cylinder engine with overhead inlet valves and side exhaust. Axe and shovel mounted on the side, open top, flat canvas driver's seat, left-hand drive.

The live axle on leaf springs made it ideal for the washed-out tarmac roads and sand-scoured bush tracks trying to get through the mangroves to the beach and reef, where floods and cyclones and monsoons riled up the crocodiles and extended invitations to the cane toads. We often took our jeep out to the coast so we could cool down in the tepid, slow-moving sea, and then ended up digging, winching, pushing, covered in sand and mud, cursing inelegantly for overextending the little vehicle's capabilities.

But, that morning we were on the Bruce Highway, out of Townsville, heading north. In the front passenger seat, my girlfriend was stripped to her knickers, sunbaking through the windscreen and the open top. She had thrown her clothes, shirt, trousers, bra and socks, piece by piece, into the back footwell behind her seat, then, as they rose and filled with air, threatening to fly out behind us, she tossed her heavy, non-tropical Doc Martens over her shoulder on to the floor to weigh them down.

Bare feet up on the dash locker handle, she had ABBA and Stevie Nicks down on air guitar, then air keyboard, crescendo, riffs and licks, knowing she could be famous; head banging, seat dancing, singing any of the words she could remember, making up new ones in the gaps ...

Two things happened.

A muscular tarantula ran up from the disturbed safety of the back footwell, where it had been cowering under her pile of clothes, across her leg and on up the inside of the front windshield. There it gripped with its toes and right on the top edge, leaned into the wind. My reaction was immediate and not pretty, using clutch and brake and accelerator at random. The brake marks we left on the hot bitumen later became legend, with random people from the bar driving out from town to take photos with their Kodaks. But this came later.

A police car pulled out behind us from an overgrown cutting on a side road, lights flashing, and came up dangerously close to our backend. The officer gestured unmistakably that we should pull over.

My first instinct, indicated by prior experience of the police, was to avoid stopping until my passenger found her clothes and got dressed in the front seat, but, given the spider situation, I was already onto the loose edge of the road shoulder and skidding to a stop.

At this point, my girlfriend was frozen in horror at the spider, the rock and roll as we swung at speed off the bitumen into soft gravel, and the ominous appearance of the police officer, who was by then out of his car, settling his broad-brimmed hat onto his head and walking purposefully towards us. He was tall, six foot six, or more, and, as he loomed over the open top of the low-slung jeep, he cast a black shadow of doom over our excursion.

Ladies. How ya goin'? Can I help yous? said the police officer, leaning across my girlfriend's naked body, flicking the spider off the windscreen as an afterthought. He only has eyes for the instrument panel, the wire thin steering wheel, fold-down front windscreen, insect eyes side mirrors. *What model is this? M38 or CJ-38?*

there's a shed load of pigs out there

my cousins took me pig hunting There's a shed load of pigs out there, big ones,
it's National Park land, illegal as hell   I was eight   they were twelve and eleven
aunts and uncles were in the back yard dark, around the fire pit, not minding us
as always, they had tinnies, family grudges, schadenfreude, vindications to hash out

the cousins took their dad's truck, rolled it down the driveway, no noise and no lights
rifles wrapped in hessian bags clamped in the back, a big bastard of a spotlight
three uncontrollable yellow-eyed pig dogs, berserk with anticipation, skidding around the
back-tray   slobber   dog-stink   filthy breath   teeth

mountain gullies, washouts, low scrub, high trees, rotting logs   roaring, bucking, rearing,
braking—grunt and squeal of running pigs—chasing boys, curses, yodelling dogs, gunshots!
in the truck I crouch on the floor, ear on the cadence of the engine, listening for warning
coughs and splutters   pressing on the accelerator, to keep the spotlight on

cousins straggle back, already rehearsing the size of the pigs, how many, so close and nearly
no blood on their skinning knives, no grunt and heave of a dead pig into the truck tray
no scent of death or dying, just the smell of discharged shot, boy bodies sweat, desperate
energy, thrilling, running, the chase   stretching, falling, sidestepping, dodging, weaving

afterwards, there was a keeping to the dark edges of the house to avoid a thrashing   boys
and dogs and an eight-year-old girl had been where they shouldn't
I never saw a pig alive or dead, never saw the mountain or the swamp, only the inside of the
cabin and a cone of light cutting into nothing

the morals saver muscles

The muscle we girls needed is known as the *adductor*, a muscle located in the thigh, used for moving the legs towards the midline, and bringing the knees together. *Gracilis* is also an adductor and this one is sometimes called the anti-rape muscle or custodian of virginity! Another useful muscle in this vicinity is the *vastus medialis obliquus* or tear drop muscle.

Our boyfriends maintained a strong interest in the ability of different girls to hold the *knees-together* pose, through events such as the drive-in movies, having a warm beer in the dark during a B&S Ball, watching TV on the couch.

And if a girl spent any time at all in the back of a shaggin' wagon, it was assumed that she had not spent any time at all on developing the physical fitness of her morals saver muscles.

With the best intentions

cane toads replace pesticides
two hundred million Queensland icons
fallen from grace, cane beetle experiment backfired
cane toads replace pesticides
butt of our jokes, purses for tourists cut from their hides
hopping south in a marathon
cane toads replace pesticides
two hundred million Queensland icons

Take it from the top

1980s Queensland, honest law was set aside
in a proliferation of police corruption
the jury and the bagmen, bookies and police all lied
1980s Queensland, honest law was set aside
Premier, Ministers, Police Commissioner all hide
even the dogs were barking prostitution
1980s Queensland, honest law was set aside
in a proliferation of police corruption

Widgie

we segued from Elvis to the Beatles, *louts* and *moral delinquents*
frequenting Kings Cross milk bars in our hundreds
bodgies and widgies,
didn't know we were the new and frightening youth
subculture

newspapers said the world is turned upside down, boys
with *long hair and unusual clothes*, girls with *short hair and unusual clothes*
this was our coming of age, our undressed hair, tight
sweaters and jeans, chiffon scarves,

brightly coloured   strangely shaped   sunglasses
we watched boys who sewed themselves into tight jeans on
the weekends, slicked back their quiffs with Brylcreem

we made allowances when they didn't quite look like James
Dean

plain clothed *Bodgies and Widgies Squad* of the Victorian
Police watched us,
as our own Silver Bodgie made it into the seriously adult
lout-tolerant public sphere

Red boots

strutting the floor in her flash red boots
thumbs in her belt, she's the line dance queen
she's a mover, she's a shaker, she's getting all the looks
strutting the floor in her flash red boots
she's high on the swing and the sweat, hips loose
dust rising on the stamp of a hundred Cuban heels
strutting the floor in her flash red boots
thumbs in her belt, she's the line dance queen

Sugar and mangoes

I listen to summer season jazz, drink exotic holiday coffee, dream my way through novels with unlikely and less-than-gripping plots. The sugar is harvested, seasonal workers gone, leaving us lonely. Burdekin mangoes drop, lusciously ripe, into long grass—juiced energy for the heat of December summer.

in May
sugarcane will arrow
in flower
not for domestic display—
signalling time passing

Year of the rat

Just to be clear—I'm not thinking *Rattus rattus, that black-coated, black-hearted ratting out, snitching, authority informing, telling on, sinking ship jumping, or just jumping-ship-when-the-wind-turns rat, cunning as a dunny-rat rat,* old world-disease-sharing, *Ratsak-attracting rat, inspiration for innovative rodent control solutions.*

No, I do not give a rat's arse for *Rattus rattus.*

It's my Fussy, *Rattus fuscipes,* who does it for me, besties forever. Rounded, softest ears, chubby, fade-into-the-background grey, not cunning or too clever for her own good, but still, a quick thinker and successful, an indigenous survivor. She appears like a shadow at falling dark, slips up the veranda from her burrow near the step footing. Never demanding, reliable, a companionable foraging in the garden or under the outdoor table. We both thrill when she finds nectar, we both look away when her messy eating leaves traces of husks and pods—

She's a girl with issues

1.

most extreme dive ever
eleven kilometres into Mariana Trench
deepest point of the Pacific
finds a new species
of plastic bag

2.

if our peacenik personae
take the line of least resistance
Ohm's law dictates
we must equal evil's strength—
not steel, but bamboo

3.

when she left
I felt an obligation
of memory—
managing the accuracy
of reflection on water

making something into nothing

she never says her partner's name
contorts the language and her weekend news
avoids the pronoun that signifies, specifies   gender
pronouns keep her singular
relegate a somebody to a nobody

By-standing

Look for something tiny, something we were taught to believe is infinite.

The poets write about this: infinity in drops of water, in grains of sand. Rub the grit of a grain of sand against the softest skin you have, your underarm, inner thigh.

Catch the water molecule, multiplied into drops of rain, on your tongue. Taste for salt, the particle of salt that encouraged the molecules to collect and the drop to form.

Collect the grains of sand, build your house on them.

Collect the water molecules into channels away from the river with gates and pumps.

Keep tasting for the presence of salt.

Mix the sand with cement and water and build four hundred and sixty-seven concrete mega cities, and then build five hundred and ninety-eight extremely large cities. And keep mixing sand and cement to build the satellite towns-in-waiting, villages, roads, gutter kerbing, factories. Follow the grain of sand.

Follow the water molecule as it dashes itself desperately against the concrete, washes uselessly down the storm run-off, unable to find the earth.

At this point, count the sand, number the water. You know the word that eludes you is 'finite'.

Chicken litter

fat bodies rock, I know, whales breach and beach, lemmings run, leap, fall—

walking on concrete malevolence breaks joints, stretches ligaments, jars minds

where the whole earth breaks through, we are tempted to walk, all the down treads of all humans ever, is absorbed to spring us back up, to step again

our boots have never trod lightly, cement points to where we should walk, hides the individuality of our tracks, dissuades us from straying from the agreed-on path

so, in the face of the collapse of Western civilisation, a KFC litterer is hardly notice that the sky is falling in the night-time, lemmings are leaping, whales beaching

the litterer walks along our street, strays over into our garden,   stuffs KFC litter, chicken-pieces tub, paper bag, waxed cup   into our wattle bush

Class grudge

Her grandma has the super, both her mums work two jobs. Her work future's a forever of looking grimly into serial contracts, part-time weeks, staggered shifts. When the bosses need her, checking her rostered availability, she goes in.

It all starts badly, red sauce from the squirty bottle splatted vindictively on the front of her nearly white shirt, clogging the buttons, sticking in the tailored buttonholes and *bloody hell,* dropping before she could catch it, onto the pristine white canvas of the pride of her sartorial efforts, the Dunlop volleys. And no-one at the truck stop gives her a second look.

It was too soon. Her joke at the water cooler, a bit sardonic, a bit ironic, very funny. No-one laughed. There was eye rolling between the boss's son and the cashier's daughter, designer jeans and high heeled boots, *Like, what was that? Did she speak?*

She asks them *How clever did you have to be to get a job in your father's truck stop café?*

Leaving her secondary school in a distant valley, she travelled the red dust roads until they turned to bitumen, to the B-string University town. She picked fruit, packed fruit, lateraled tobacco, picked tobacco and sewed it on to hangers for the drying sheds, her hands stained with the sticky brown nicotine, lining her cuticles and staining her lifelines and palm patterns.

So where is this going? Remember the joke at the water cooler? She comes from a long lineage of thin-skinned, grudge-bearing, quick-to-take-offence, disappointment-seekers. And you should know this, take every opportunity to pick up hints and strategies modelled by your elders. Check them out now, gathered around the breakfast table, just starting on the toast and corn flakes. It's any nothing-to-worry-about Spring day, sun shining, magpies, bottlebrushes flowering, warm bread steaming, jam, fresh brewed coffee aroma-ing. Her ancestors, to make the day complete, to fill in the missing piece, can pull from forty-year storage a grudge held in readiness, shine it off on a shirt sleeve, hold it up for all those at the table to scrutinise for worthiness ... a grudge still good, no use-by date, well-kept, and well worth the keeping.

This handed-down character dimension, through the generations, is particularly useful and satisfying when a long-term relationship is uncomfortably achieving perfection (or close enough to be alarming). We cannot help ourselves, enhance it with a thin-skinned absorption of slight, embellish with a description of a disappointment imagined. And keep the grudge, ready for review, as long as it takes, a lifetime of usefulness.

So, just saying, those two at the water cooler, she can let them wait, let them stew, keep them checking over their shoulders ...

this city is gay and cool to me

do you remember when passers-by hissed and spat
at us in the mall and cat
calls followed us when we linked arms
looked into the faces of the boy gangs outside the bars
walked away laughing, high on the heat of revolution?
can you recall when we knew our bodies were the sacrifice,
being out and gay a high risk to the world's moral fibre?
remember, we celebrated equality in 2017 with new rainbow
number plates minted in the year of the plebiscite—
now this city is gay and cool to me, no cadastral map
acknowledges an ancient ownership
nor the nine shades of blue in the Brindabellas.
Painting a roundabout on a Braddon street in rainbows
is not just gay but seriously *gay*, do the interjectors who
think that's cool but are maybe not so cool, have no memory
of my struggle, ignorant of my history, that they voted for
or against on my behalf … cool and gay is more
than swings and roundabouts, more than a going around
and coming around, a being around
your votes can send us back to the fists of our urgent
histories where we are at once at stake
where gay is serious, cool is compliance, and evil
is so banal we do not see it coming.

Swarm

words are poison   they wake the 'swarm'—
it stirs

the words we use are on *our* heads—
come back to bite us

swarm
in flight   outraged   fights
back.   streets erupt

provoked. Now police are insects
toxic   harm

world peace is one decision away

The unexpected power of underarm hair reveals itself with the unselfconscious wing uplift, seen to best advantage on the four am cleaning shift at a suburban Coles. We mop the fruit and veg aisle, haul the heavy metal industrial polisher up and down the grey glazed lino of the sticky drinks aisle, doing things to make that floor shine that we never think to do at home. On the shelves, lamington cake in cellophane, Flo's home-made pumpkin scones, wagon wheels and Liquorice All-Sorts. And even the non-exotic foodstuffs like fruit and nuts, biscuits and cheese, flown in from Brazil or California or Amsterdam.

It was the time of Dusty Springfield's teased blonde bouffant and not generally a good time for hats. We cut our own hair ourselves and leave it to go its own way.

And we think we are all sorts of radical, because we are over the peroxide and bleach and Magic Silver White, so the armpit hair revealed by the sleeveless T-shirts and singlets is a shocker, the dark tangle outing the peroxide blondes with its dankness and mystery.

In the tropic heat, if we are not careful, our armpits fall easily into deodorant-clogged rankness, tropical mould and strange growths of scunge.

You're not doing yourselves any favours said my mother

But after the second thoughts, self-doubt, the prickles and stubble of the growing out, armpit hair, washed soft in rainwater, is comforting as fur, oddly pleasing to the stroking finger tips ...

the police do not intervene

veins under her sunmarked skin, lifting blue like maps of inland watercourses, attracting colours red, yellow, green,

tattoos on the side of her neck pulse   glow   reaching around in tendrils to grasp her throat

the crowd leans in, all their voices blending in one anticipatory bloom of abusive satisfaction

police cordons, more uniforms than protestors, arms linked across both ends of the intersection

torn cardboard signs   red lettering   broken wooden stakes   all bleed into the gutter in the downpour

the crowd waits, wanting action, wanting anything, pushed forward from behind.

the police do not intervene

Rising

this is how it will be

sand   hills   sandhills   wind
silica sharp   abrading skin like a cheese grater
wind   sand   wind

scarf ends whipping   face covered   clothes anchored to the body with one
clenched hand

this is how it will be

keeping a tomato plant alive
with dregs from a thousand drinks of tea
at every sunrise and every sunset   cup by cup
plant by plant

a feral cat drinks only blood
nests in the heights of a dead tree eyrie
feasts on parrots, denudes the desert
lizard by lizard

no use for words like
lush verdant soaking
no longer in common usage   luxuriant   fecund   fertile   rich
flood   rain   floodplain (no use unless qualified as catastrophic)

bees
frogs
blue blues all the blues
by mutual consent red river gums relinquish life, and, in one suicide pact, die
river-beds shrivelling with rustling, rasping dead cicada wings
broken steamers stranded high on the banks like failed Arks
wait for the 100-year flood, every ten years

camels wander the streets dreaming of water
in the bottom of the swales remembrance of green
delicacy of grey whispering grasses   stone by stone abrading
sand dunes rising higher

sea dragged higher by every rising moon
desert moving east on each rising wind
scarcity causing not only words to fail

this is how it will be

The 'dismantle' triolets

you really want me to ask forgiveness
for poetry too direct and graphic
poems saying *lesbian* are too unambiguous
you really want me to ask forgiveness?
your canon shrivels avoiding the obvious,
words too unrestrained, too undiplomatic
you really want me to ask forgiveness
for poetry too direct and graphic?

you really want lesbians to ask forgiveness
for poetry too direct and graphic—
it's too telling, the politics, the bluntness
you really want lesbians to ask forgiveness
for saying what's real, and not fictitious?
it's all too much for you, far too explicit
you really want lesbians to ask forgiveness
for poetry too direct and graphic?

you really want us to ask forgiveness
for poetry too direct and graphic—
poets' tools dismantling masters' houses
you really want us to ask forgiveness?
your straight man's canon has little now to give us
can't talk truth to power with dissembling poetics
you really want us to ask forgiveness
for poetry too direct and graphic?

you really want women to ask forgiveness
for poetry too direct and graphic—
your disapproval and exclusion keep our voices diminished
you really want women to ask forgiveness?
silencing us is what you did to witches
whether poetry or prose, the difference is not specific
you really want women to ask forgiveness
for poetry too direct and graphic?

Revolution

the revolution of 1863
Singer sewing machines and Butterick/McCall's patterns collected in Lever arch files

made fashion available to us all
gave us Pattern 6015   the 'walk away' dress   in standard graded sizes   patterned in

tissue paper for folding and shipping
collect it in your letter box from the morning mail   wear it to the city at lunchtime

Bedding

when I was courting I went for
white sheets   heavy cotton
doona cover   pillowcases   all white   all matching   'a set'
hospital corners   sheet turned down   spray of flowers   chocolate
very *House and Garden*   very *Women's Weekly*

the object of my courting didn't notice

bed at her place a random collection of quilts, doonas, mismatched blankets,
eiderdowns, discarded hoodies   a dog's breakfast   so to speak   in fact, a
dog's bed with dog treasures cached under the pillows and heavy wafts of dog in
the random rucks of unmade sheets

looking temporary   as if   she's only staying a short while   even in her own
space

one morning she and the dog will wake under a hedge   in a sleeping fug of
body warmth some place   on their way   to another bed

Traps

my mother had little love for cardigans

sometimes, coiled around her neck, she wore a plaited leather stockwhip used
for moving the bulls, some lengths of baling twine or fencing wire to make
necessary repairs
when we rode out to check the traps

curse of rabbits
skins stripped inside out
their soft, soft fur

Lesbian content

I am employed as *Lesbian Content* to tick boxes demonstrating "gender and sexuality friendliness". The tick is a small self-satisfied noise in HR Recruitment. *Job Done!*

I silently lesbian in coffee machine clusters, water cooler leaning, and staff meeting tables.

Silently lesbianing at a hot desk in open plan Department of Everything. Lesbianing without comment at staff barbeques and *Fun Run, Government is of the people* days.

This job is a silent one. No ostentatious, obvious raising of LGBTIQAAA+ issues, themes or words to complicate the normal routines and outputs. Just a brooding, accusatory, no-noise presence—*I'm watching you, and listening in.*

Moscow is just a state of mind

Seen from our earth (note the possessive tenor of my thinking) the Moon is covered with plains of basalt, cooled lava making dark surfaces, which we, in our naiveté, believe in and name as Seas: Sea of Tranquillity, Serenitatis, Fecunditatis, Vaporum, Humorum, Crisium … all these *States of Mind*.

And Moscoviense? Sea of Moscow? On the Moon, Moscow is a state of mind.

You ask me to believe in the hidden world of atoms with no evidence available to my earth-educated eye; take *atoms* on faith like a primitive, religious system, as we once believed in the Seas on the Moon.

And then the atomic bomb. We saw it at Hiroshima and at the Woomera testing site. This was something real, to give substance to our faith in atoms. Nine devastating atomic bomb trials in post-WWII Cold War paranoia. We thought the world was both with us and against us.

See the moonscape of Lake Hart and the Maralinga Tjarutja lands.

planting flags
buying naming rights
are they playing a long game
claiming the Moon for Moscow?

Munga-Thirri

Federation drought, 1900: the last desert people walked out of Munga-Thirri,
of the sand hill country, they knew themselves as Wangkangurru.
From inside the desert, out into the unknown, what they see first is the fence.
On nearby dunes a camel walks across the moon—sounding camel bells
call up a sky of stars, galaxies held just above the dust by hakea.
Two boys dreaming maps the journey, desert stories and stars, to mikiri.

Corkwood trees, *Hakea eyreana*, surround the water wells. From mikiri to mikiri,
we know time is pointless when we walk the story through Munga-Thirri.
Spinifex grows outwards in circles, uses time to die off in the centre; hakea
bark burned to white ash for their wounds, can't salve the hurt of Wangkangurru.
Some nights sadness is sung by dingoes, singing to the camel bells,
and in the breaking silence, futility intrudes, there in the line of the fence.

All the ones who walked the dunes, not knowing the constraint of the fence,
know water is survival-mapped. In the campsite at the mikiri,
voices, Pashtun, Baloch, Sindhi, carry from the breakfast fire, soft as camel bells.
Their work was stringing wire for the vermin fence, on the edge of Munga-Thirri,
but now the fence lies buried under moving sand, no interest to Wangkangurru:
800 ks through gidgee bush, cane grass on a dune crest, thickets of hakea,

wadi trees, acacia peuce, coolabahs, through swales alive with hakea.
Colonising sand dunes, even before the wire was strung, rabbits beat the fence.
But the desert space is known through the skin of Wangkangurru,
and dust plumes over silent plaques marking the place of a once lost mikiri.
Dingo steps, stops, fades, watches from the swale edge in Munga-Thirri,
muezzin crow calls sunrise, grazing herd drifts after timeless camel bells.

Wind blows and gusts, setting a whisper through the grasses, underscored by camel
bells,
camp-fire scorching seeds like roasted almonds, sweet nectar, solace of hakea.
Government draws a line on paper to fix in time the boundary of Munga-Thirri,
although time here moves and shifts over the line that was once a fence.
Dust veils the sunrise, clouds the trees, layers the hidden places of mikiri,
shadowing ghosts walking north to pitjuri fields through the country of
Wangkangurru.

The People of this desert country know themselves as Wangkangurru.
Straying through and over dunes, the herd is mapped by camel bells.
Two boys dreaming, rainmakers' songs, story-maps the mikiri.
Cameleers and Wangkangurru take as commonplace the marvel of the hakea.
Scientists walk transect surveys with camels, cross curiously over the boundary fence.
Two boys dreaming seeps into the body, consuming whoever walks into Munga-Thirri.

Look for signs: two boys dreaming, the mikiri of the Wangkangurru...
as you walk Munga-Thirri country, listen as well for camel bells,
deep in a swale of hakea, when you cross the abandoned fence.

Mungo

since I have known the flat lands you came from I have wondered through
winter nights what you want that keeps you there—forty thousand year
old bones of the People, gathered through time as the lake edge moves,
water turning to salt crust, wind creating dune from earth, paths through
night-cold sand in desert scrub changing direction under footfalls without
footprint—

wondered what silent, sacred knowledge bonds you to this dry earth, mined
and tracked by bandicoots and tiny desert mice, echidna and dunnart

smallest known mammalian Y chromosome in the body of a tiny mouse-sized
marsupial

those nights I wondered why the sigh when you pull up home in the rusted
ute, kill the engine, sit with hands on wheel, hat pushed back and eyes
reclaiming, after every trip to town, the horizon, and all country up to its
haze and boundary ...

Playing us

The fire tracks us for days along the city's edge,
like a wild camel on the dune-top, shadowing our movements, waiting for the moment
to maraud and rampage in amongst our domestic smallness,

our bush capital, a recent discordant note in historical time
settlers unsettled in the territory of fire, trespassing in a place claimed by flame
burning takes its own time, plays its own game forever, makes its own weather

Emissaries of smoke are sent on each wind change,
it glows malevolent on satellite maps, taunts, turns burning fingers towards us,
then pulls away, back to the wilderness where we cannot follow

leaves us breathless, waiting, for the next turn, the next heat spike.
It plays, we tense, it threatens, we watch, it runs and storms, we retreat
Days pass … still it tracks along the western hills, looks down on our intruder city.

Smoke covers the streets and houses, enters every breathing body,
camps out in hair and carpets, hangs between us and the sun, *my fire is out there* it says,
stringing out our dread, playing us, a game of nerves

Rain

months of false forecasts
at last the clouds deliver
stalks and stems unfold
we check maps, predictions
greedy for more

one day we're wilting
in 40-degree heat
stifling smoke haze,
then overnight the deluge—
we complain about raincoats

even in rain
curlews and currawongs
are busy
humans cry about the drought
complain about the Wet

in drought-breaking rain
the bush changes colour
smells rich and alive
wet kangaroos chew new shoots—
just add water

Water the colour of tea

water the colour of tea
searches behind the leveé for
possibilities
joeys, never known rain, their ears full
of mist
are all eyes and twitch

cane toads spawning tadpoles in the
wheel tracks behind the machinery shed
destined to hop south, puddle by
puddle

Thinking about you

Hi Eye KSJ,

So pleased to see your tag again. The last time I knew you were around was up near the roundabout on the power box a couple of months ago. Glad you made it through the coronavirus lockdown ok. I was worried. Not sure if you have a good place to social distance in, or wash your hands enough, or even if tag artists take that kind of thing seriously. I've seen your tag around for a year or so, which means you are not too far away. That one on the wall of the storm drain was a beauty, but it has been painted over. Probably by the JobSeeker crowd doing community work for their pandemic payment.

But this tag is new and fresh, so I think you must be out and about and feeling pretty good. And have made it through. Good to see a familiar presence again on my morning walk. It's been a bit lonely at the house with no visitors allowed and only saying a quick hello to the postie (who has a new electric bike now, have you seen them? ... no warning that they're on the street so I have to be a bit nippy to get out to the box in time).

It was a bit of a shock to be lumped in with the 'nearly dead' by the US President, but we have to stay up-beat I think, look for the good things in life. We'll be dead long enough.

I check the 'heaven spot' at the top of the water tank back of Hackett sometimes to see if you've been back there. And I'm glad you haven't. It's far too dangerous. Crumbling, slippery, too high. Nothing to hold on to.

Also, a heads up if you have any wet-cement-art mates ... there are new footpaths being laid in Watson at the end of May, an infrastructure project to keep Canberrans working through COVID-19. If you keep an eye out there will be lots of pristine wet concrete available ... tabula rasa, so to speak ... and it's a pity to just leave it to the kids on bikes to make a mark.

Looking forward to your next tag, stay safe, wash your hands,
Public servant (retired)

Content warning: biggest reduction in the noise of human activity as natural noise is heard again above seismic noise

I stay at home, the whole world drops away
Go out, the whole world's in my face
Seismic noise keeps natural sounds at bay
Noise that meant my life went all one way
when you look like that you're just a waste of space
I stay at home, the whole world drops away
Girls are forced to notice fear when they
refuse to go out dressed in bows and lace
Seismic noise keeps natural sounds at bay
Blokes say your look's an invite, they must go all the way
My fists are clenched around the can of Mace
I stay at home, the whole world drops away
In overalls I'm held up to the light of day
Blundstone boots are armour, a body's carapace
Seismic noise keeps natural sounds at bay
Disparagement and frowns did not hold sway
I stand my ground in how I take up space
I stay at home, the whole world drops away
Seismic noise keeps natural sounds at bay

Chopping wood as an antidote to failed expectations in regard to the search for a life-partner

I raise the axe, it's high above my head
My shoulders tense, my eye locks in a sight-line
I sigh, and slowly lower it instead
Chopping wood's a task I've come to dread
I only do it when relationships decline
I raise the axe, it's high above my head
It's all my fault, I'm taking that as read
Having tickets on yourself, a bar that's high, is fine
I sigh, and slowly lower it instead
It's not as though we made it to your bed
Or that we even had a 'thing' to pine
I raise the axe, it's high above my head
You're up yourself if you think I'm easily led
but my hand and yours held high the wine
I sigh, and slowly lower it instead
I'm pretty sure it's the Universe, not something that I said
but you getting paralytic drunk was probably a sign
I raise the axe, it's high above my head
I sigh, and slowly lower it instead

Afterword

In 1979 Audre Lorde said 'those of us who stand outside the circle of this society's definition of acceptable women [need to learn] how to take our differences and make them strengths. For the master's tools will never dismantle the master's house'. (Audre Lorde, *History Is a Weapon: The Master's Tools Will Never Dismantle the Master's House,* 1979)

As a woman, lesbian and poet I frequently find myself standing outside the acceptable. In this collection I use a range of traditional poetry forms to lay bare some of the gaping fault-lines of gender relations especially as they are experienced by LGBTIQ communities.

The forms, or the master's tools, include triolet, sestina, pantoum, tanka prose, tanka, prose poetry, micro-lit, story and free form poems. The content ranges freely in time from the 1950s to the present day, from the contemporary to memoir, gender politics, bushfires and floods. It contains jeeps, trucks, girlfriends and canecutters, widgies, Singer sewing machines, rats and class grudges. There are poems here about dissent and resistance, social revolutions, outrage and anger, to expand the canon of femininities. There is reflection here, and also, love poems.

These poems feature our LGBTIQ presence in the world. I've written these poems with the full intention of upsetting the order of the social order. Gender and sexuality are important because they are such complex and defining features of our lives and personalities. There is no escaping them. If the reader (however they define or perform or express their sexuality) reads the poems, and at the same time inhabits them as they were written, by a lesbian, then the edifices of the 'acceptable' will be dismantled, undressed and exposed. Inhabit my words with your gender fluid sensibility.

Notes

There's a love story here FNQ Far North Queensland

Burdekin snow Burdekin snow is ash from burning cane blowing across the region.

Take it from the top The Commission of Inquiry into Possible Illegal Activities and Associated Police Misconduct (the Fitzgerald Inquiry; 1987–1989) into Queensland Police corruption was a judicial inquiry presided over by Tony Fitzgerald QC. The inquiry resulted in the resignation of the Premier (head of government), the calling of two by-elections, the jailing of three former ministers and the Police Commissioner (who also lost his knighthood). It also contributed to the end of the National Party of Australia's 32-year run as the governing political party in Queensland. (Wikipedia).

Widgie Bob Hawke in public life from 1956, in Parliament from 1980, was known as the Silver Bodgie.

Year of the Rat *Rattus fuscipes:* Native bush rat.

if our peacenik personae Ohm's law—Substance or device opposes the passage of electric current causing energy disruption. Resistance is equal to the voltage divided by the current.

This city is gay and cool to me Hannah Arendt on the banality of evil.

The 'dismantle' triolets In December 2019 during the US election debates candidates were asked if they would rather ask forgiveness or give a gift. All the men said they would give a gift. The two women said they would ask forgiveness for being too direct, too blunt, too forceful, too passionate. Source: 'The 2020 Democrats were told to give a gift or ask for forgiveness: Guess what the women chose', *New York Times,* 20 November 2019.

In 1979 Audre Lorde said 'those of us who stand outside the circle of this society's definition of acceptable women [need to learn] how to take our differences and make them strengths. For the master's tools will never dismantle the master's house'. Source: *History Is a Weapon: The Master's Tools Will Never Dismantle the Master's House,* Audre Lorde, 1979.

Munga-Thirri Munga-Thirri/Simpson Desert, Australia.

The submission of this poem for publication is supported by Don Rowlands OAM, Wangkangurru Yarluyandi elder, QPWS Senior Ranger for the Munga-Thirri.

Acknowledgements

Thanks to my poetry workshop group (Moya Pacey, Kerrie Nelson, Hazel Hall, Rosa O'Kane, Sue Peachey), who have been supportive and encouraging, above and beyond.

Thanks to the Canberra community of poets, generous individuals of which, have provided opportunity, participative and inclusive space, place and venues, and collegiate acknowledgement.

Thanks to Shane Strange, who embodies all the above qualities.

Thanks to Beth and Nigel at Smith's Alternative for their support for poetry making.

Thanks to Tikka, who accesses the mysteries and horrors of publishing technology and internet with charm and grace.

Some of the poems have been previously published:

'Legs' in *Australian Poetry Anthology*, Sara Saleh and Melinda Smith (eds), 8, 2020

'There's a shed load of pigs out there' in *Mountain Secrets Anthology*, Joan Fenney (ed.), Ginninderra Press, 2019

'The morals saver muscles' in Spineless Wonders, 2019 joanne burns Microlit Award, longlist for inclusion in a range of multi-platform activities including #storybombingNWF20, podcasts, live performance and the Microflix Awards.

'Widgie' in *Other Terrain*, Anne Casey (ed.), 8, 2019

'Red Boots' in *The Blue Nib*, 40, Winter 2020

'Sugar and mangoes' in *Contemporary Haibun Online*, Tish Davis (ed.), 16, no.1, 2020

'Year of the Rat' in *The Blue Nib*, 40, Winter 2020

'most extreme dive ever' in *Ribbons*, David Rice (ed.), 15, no. 3, Fall 2019

'if our peacenik personae' in Turn the Other Cheek: Nonviolent Resistance and Peaceful Protest Tanka, *Atlas Poetica*, Autumn Noelle Hall (ed.), 2019

'when she left' in *Skylark Tanka*, Clare Everett (ed.), 13, Summer 2019

'Making something into nothing' in *Westerly* 64, no.1, July 2019

'This city is gay and cool to me' in *I Protest: Poems of Dissent*, Stephen Matthews (ed.), Ginninderra Press 2020

'The police do not intervene' in *Right Now: Human Rights in Australia*, 29, November 2019

'Rising' in *Right Now: Human Rights in Australia*, 29, October 2019

'Revolution' in *Backstory,* Anne Casey (ed.), 8, 2019

'Bedding', *The Blue Nib*, 40, Winter 2020

'Traps' in *The Blue Nib*, 40, Winter 2020

'lesbian content' in *Shuffle anthology*, Short Australian Stories, Spineless Wonders, Cassandra Atherton (ed.), 2019

'Moscow is just a state of mind' Living in the World: Creativity, Science, Environments, *Axon Creative Explorations*, 9, no. 2, 2019

'Munga-Thirri' in *Meniscus*, 8, no. 1, 2020

'Mungo' in *Meniscus* 4, no. 2, 2016

'Playing us' in *Not Very Quiet*, Sandra Renew and Moya Pacey (eds.), 6, 2020

'Rain' in *Atlas Poetica,* 40, 2020

'Thinking about you' in Living Letters Project, *Cicerone Journal*, Rosalind Moran and Nancy Jin (eds), 2020

About the Author

Sandra Renew's work has been published internationally, nationally and locally, as hard copy and online. She has a local and national reputation as a performance poet and was a featured poet at the National Folk Festival Spoken Word for three years, from 2017 to 2019.

Sandra also writes short form prose and micro-lit and was a finalist for both the 2018 and 2019 joanne burns Microlit Award.

She is experimenting with using traditional forms to write about LGBTIQ presence in the world with the express aim of upsetting the order of the social order.

It's the sugar, Sugar is her fourth collection after *Acting Like a Girl* (Recent Work Press 2019), *The Orlando Files* (Ginninderra Press 2018) and *Who Sleeps at Night* (Ginninderra Press 2017). Sandra's collection, *Acting Like a Girl*, was the winner of the 2020 ACT Writing and Publishing Award for Poetry.

One Last Border: Poetry for refugees was co-written as a fundraising project with Hazel Hall and Moya Pacey (Ginninderra Press 2015)

Sandra is a founding editor, with Moya Pacey, of *Not Very Quiet,* an online journal for women's poetry and co-hosts the Not Very Quiet women's poetry nights at Smith's Alternative. Sandra and Moya were awarded a Canberra Critics Circle Award for their influential contribution to women's poetry in 2019.

Printed in Australia
AUHW020836040621
346631AU00002B/2